A Look in the Mirror

Freeing Yourself from the Body Image Blues

Valerie Rainon McManus, LCSW-C

Child & Family Press • Washington, DC

Child & Family Press is an imprint of the Child Welfare League of America. The Child Welfare League of America is the nation's oldest and largest membership-based child welfare organization. We are committed to engaging people everywhere in promoting the well-being of children, youth, and their families, and protecting every child from harm. All proceeds from the sale of this book support CWLA's programs in behalf of children and families.

CHILD WELFARE LEAGUE OF AMERICA, INC.
HEADQUARTERS
440 First Street, NW, Third Floor, Washington, DC 20001-2085
E-mail: books@cwla.org

CURRENT PRINTING (last digit)
10 9 8 7 6 5 4 3 2 1

Cover image courtesy of CSA Images, www.csaimages.com
Cover and text design by Amy Alick Perich
Edited by Tegan A. Culler

Printed in the United States of America

ISBN # 0–87868-897-8

Library of Congress Cataloging-in-Publication Data

McManus, Valerie Rainon.
  A look in the mirror : freeing yourself from the body image blues /
Valerie Rainon McManus.
       p. cm.
  Includes bibliographical references.
  ISBN 0-87868-897-8 (alk. paper)
 1. Body image in adolescence--Juvenile literature. 2. Body image--Social
aspects--United States--Juvenile literature. 3. Teenage girls--Health and
hygiene--Juvenile literature. 4. Teenage girls--Mental health--Juvenile
literature. 5. Self-perception in adolescence--Juvenile literature. 6.
Self-acceptance in adolescence--Juvenile literature. I. Title.
  RA777.25.M386 2004
  613'.04243--dc22
                        2004003374

Dedication

This book is dedicated to my husband, Craig.

From the time of our teenage years,

you have accompanied me on this enlightened journey,

ceaselessly fostering my growth and determination

with your insight and enthusiasm.

You challenge and inspire me to continue plowing onward,

even during times of uncertainty.

Thank you for always demonstrating your faith in me.

I am truly blessed to share life

with such a unique and beautiful spirit.

I love you!

Contents

Acknowledgments vii

Foreword: For Parents, Caregivers, and Other Caring Adults ix

Chapter 1: Introduction 1

Chapter 2: About You 3

Chapter 3: Becoming You 13

Chapter 4: Your Social World 19

Chapter 5: Societal Expectations 23

Chapter 6: The Media Message 33

Chapter 7: Women in Advertising 45

Chapter 8: Advertising: A Closer Look 51

Chapter 9: Your Self-Image .63

Chapter 10: Straight Talk About Dieting 69

Chapter 11: Drastic Measures: Eating Disorders 75

Chapter 12: Getting Help 83

Chapter 13: Healthy Living, Not Dead-End Dieting 89

Chapter 14: A Healthy Body Image 103

Chapter 15: What Makes Us Great 111

Chapter 16: Getting Over It! 125

Chapter 17: Reflections of Your True Self 129

References: For More Information 133

About the Author 139

Acknowledgments

As is true of all our accomplishments, many people share in my ability to have written this book.

Thank you to my family, who has offered unyielding support and interest. You are incredibly special people, and I am privileged to call you my family. Thank you to my parents, Dianne and Larry Lasoff; to Adam, Danny, Melanie, and Josh; to my grandparents Phyllis and Bernie Rice and Joe and Dottie Lasoff. Thanks to my aunts, uncles, and cousins, Susan, Melvin, Ivy, and Jason Bazensky; Taffy and Joe Rice; and Elaine Lasoff. Thank you to my mother- and father-in-law, Janice and Jim McManus, and to Kristen and Jen. You are such a blessing to me.

A special thank you to Jim McManus for your pride and faith. You eased my struggle through your unwavering belief that my work should be shared, and you have warmed my heart by believing in me.

Thank you to my sister, Melanie Lasoff-Levs. Since I was a small girl, I have looked to you with great pride. You offered a role model of talent, strength, and compassion. You and I share the part of our soul in which our childhood lies. I am grateful to have spent those years with you, to be able to look eagerly toward our future, and to always call you my sister.

Thank you to Patricia Flanagan for sharing my plight and passion, for offering your shoulder during difficult times, and for being someone in whose life exists an example of pure woman-power for us all to behold. You are, and always will be, one of the most beautiful blessings in my life.

To Cristine Zocchi, who has exemplified the role of mentor and so much more. The wisdom, friendship, and sense of connection you provide yielded endless inspiration and spiritual guidance. Thank you for your bravery and sisterly love.

Thank you to Nyree Wannall for your unrelenting positivity and encouragement. Through you I remember the pure delight of girlhood friendships, which are always cherished, and which never end.

To Bill and David MacCormack for offering your skills and talents whenever called upon and your friendship, always. To Gillian Diamond and Jennifer and Ethan Weinstein for bringing so much laughter and love to my life. Thank you to Willow and Tyler, whose affection and antics have always poured forth without reservation. I love you guys and all you have taught me.

To my family at Camp Louise and Camp Airy in western Maryland; there are more of you then I could ever name. Thank you for long days in the sunshine, for nights giggling together in the woods, and for helping to grow the woman inside the girl. Thank you to Sherri "Sherbear" Barber, for it is through your eyes that I am able to envision my own potential. I am so proud of you and all you are becoming.

Thank you to the entire staff of Anne Arundel County's Court Appointed Special Advocates Program, Inc. (CASA). I am honored to work with such an extraordinary group of people dedicated to bettering the lives of children in need, one child at a time.

Thank you to all of my teachers from my earliest years through high school graduation at Thomas S. Wootton in Rockville, MD. Thank you to my professors at the University of Maryland at College Park and the University of Maryland at Baltimore School of Social Work. With your own passion you opened my eyes.

To Nicole, thank you for sharing your story with me back in a quiet Denton-7 dorm room in the fall of 1992. Though our time together was short, I will never forget your face. Thank you to Shelley Nichols for reminding me of my own value through your support, openness, and loving friendship. You sincerely touched me with your beautiful spirit, and I will always remember you with deep admiration.

To Lindsey Hall-Cohn of Gürze Books, thank you for your encouragement and input and for all the passionate work you and Leigh do to combat eating disorders.

It has been a tremendous honor to work with the Child Welfare League of America and Child & Family Press. The intense commitment demonstrated by this organization to better the lives of families and children is supported by its staff's professionalism and its endless contribution of resources and activism efforts. Thank you to Eve Malakoff-Klein. I am so grateful for your interest and expertise in considering this project. My respect for you and all you do is unyielding. Great thanks to Peggy Tierney for your unrelenting vision and support, for your genuine enthusiasm and skill. A special thank you to my editor, Tegan Culler, for all of your attention to this project and for your faith in the material contained herein. Your talent, positivity, and proficiency made a world of difference in allowing this work to be all that was intended. A big thank you to all the other affiliated staff who have contributed to this project. This would not have been possible without your dedication. I am so grateful for all of your involvement.

Finally, I want to thank all of the women of this cause whose struggles, insights, and brilliance have inspired my own awakening, primarily Dr. Jean Kilbourne, Dr. Mary Pipher, and Ms. Naomi Wolf. For generations to come, your voices will be heard.

For Parents, Caregivers, and Other Caring Adults

As a young girl, I had a sense that something was not quite right with the world. Although I could not pinpoint the problem, I was definitely aware of one main characteristic: It existed in the lives of women. Due to my inability to define this phenomenon, I did not have the tools I needed to arm myself against its potentially devastating nature. *A Look in the Mirror* was designed to be this missing resource for young women, helping them to identify the harmful messages impacting their development so they might become educated decisionmakers, choosing a life of health and happiness rather then one of self-loathing and destruction.

Like most American girls, I became attuned early in life to the high standards of beauty and thinness expected of women in our culture, and the intense importance imparted to these traits. These messages came from endless elements of my social environment, including television programs, magazines, advertisements, family members, peers, and so forth.

Upon entering puberty, my figure naturally began to take on a more womanly shape. Like many of my female peers, I began to diet to combat this sudden increase in body fat. As my body started to require more calories for proper growth, I allowed it less. So began an almost constant internal war, either depriving myself of food or chastising and belittling myself for giving in to my body's desire for it. With newfound fixations on appearance and weight management, my previous interests in athletics, art, and math took a back seat, and I certainly was not alone.

As a result of this struggle, my self-esteem plummeted during my teenage years, my head full of magazine models, television actresses, and movie stars whose images of perfection made me feel like a complete failure. Many of the adult women in my life made frequent references to their own body dissatisfaction while encouraging me to lose weight. By the time I graduated from high school, weight loss was a familiar focal point in my life.

Entering college was a transition of great excitement as well as one of anxiety. My own unresolved childhood difficulties began to resurface, complicating things further and leaving me feeling vulnerable and powerless. At the same time, I encountered an onslaught of college women fixated on their appearance. Because we lived with one another, our various means of unhealthy dieting bombarded us more heavily than ever. The dorm hallways were saturated with girls whose attitudes and behaviors were a direct reflection of body-weight obsession.

Before long, the intensity of my own dieting increased dramatically. The combination of my vulnerable emotional state and the intensified pressures of body perfection created a shift inside me. I began limiting my food intake to fat-free frozen yogurt and an occasional bagel from the dining hall. Feeding myself made me guilt-ridden, and depriving myself made me feel proud and accomplished. My exercise regimen doubled. I lost 10 pounds in less then two weeks. I was tired and irritable, depressed and anxious. All the while I received compliments from family and friends about how great I looked. It was exactly the affirmation I needed to work toward more extreme measures of weight loss, and I was prepared to do just that.

Fortunately, two very special people in my life took the first step toward stopping me: my close friend, Gillian, and my future husband, Craig. They both had the courage to confront me about the changes they had observed in my eating as well as my increasingly negative attitude about my body. In desperation, Craig proposed a bottom line: "Either agree to talk to someone at the counseling center or I will *do it for you*." I was furious and mortified, but I went. It was not until some time later that I could thank him.

Despite the support that the student-group counseling provided, it was through a different experience that I finally uncovered the mysterious "something" that was wrong with the world. On a cool spring day, sitting in a lecture hall for my *Sociology of Gender* course, I reached a moment of clarity as never before. The professor began by describing the expectations of beauty for women in American society. She demonstrated how unrealistic, unhealthy, and unattainable they were. She went on to point out that our culture values women based on superficial physical attributes while ignoring the other more significant gifts and characteristics that women possess. She then explained that these messages kept women preoccupied with an unachievable and unimportant goal rather then promoting and encouraging their true power and potential. And this, she explained, was a blatant form of oppression.

In that moment, the curtain in front of my eyes was forever lifted. I clearly remember the feeling of excitement tingling over my skin as I exited the building. It was as though I had just been set free. Now that I could identify what had been suffocating me all of these years, I could consciously reject its harmful messages and resist my own oppression. I floated across campus to meet Craig and promptly announced to him, "I am a feminist!"

Almost immediately my fixation shifted from body obsession to gender studies. I devoured the required readings and sought out additional materials at the library. I read excerpts from Naomi Wolf's *The Beauty Myth* aloud as if reciting a mantra. When the semester ended, I asked my professor to supervise me for a summer project so that I could continue my study of gender issues; she graciously agreed. It soon became my deepest desire to join the field of social work where I could actively pursue positive social and political change, fighting the oppression of others in all its various forms. My college education took on a whole new meaning. I was not only grooming myself for a career, I was feeding a fire.

Several years later as a social worker, it became apparent to me that a much-needed resource on body image issues among young women was missing from the literature. While educational books were available, the girls I encountered in my work were hungry for a creative outlet that went beyond standard "reading"—they wanted to *interact*. I began writing activity sheets, creative assignments, and information pages through which the girls could explore the issues at hand with guidance, wisdom, and support, while taking an active role in their own learning.

A Look in the Mirror was written to empower girls by encouraging them to draw, to write, to make connections to their own lives and interests, and to record their own stories. Through a creative forum, young women are encouraged to examine some of the most prominent issues affecting their daily lives while making them a critical element in their own learning. Readers use their imagination and experiences to explore topics such as social environment, the influence of mass culture, media and advertising messages, body image development, disordered eating, components of healthy living, self-advocacy, and the steps to achieving a positive body image. The result is a workbook that truly promotes empowerment, health, and positivity.

The years I spent harming my body and feeling unworthy were jagged stepping-stones, sharp and unstable. Still, the experience ultimately led me in the right direction, making it possible for me to climb over the mountainside and enter into the green valley below.

While most of us cannot be expected to have only positive feelings about ourselves all of the time, body image dissatisfaction, and the harmful behaviors and attitudes associated with it, are emphatically *not* a necessary part of female development. Rather, they are the destructive and sometimes even fatal effects of a culture polluted with harmful and irresponsible messages about how women are to be valued.

It is my hope that this book will become a preventative resource for young women, helping them learn to view their world from an educated perspective of awareness, rather then one of blind acceptance. Maybe it will ease their climb up the mountainside, making those steppingstones smoother, safer, and more secure right from the start. Armed with a newfound awareness, may girls learn to shed that which distracts them from focusing on their true potential. For me, it is then that the green valley on the other side of the mountain will really be sweet.

chapter 1

Introduction

Why a Body Image Workbook?

When you look in the mirror, does your reflection make you feel confident and relaxed, or anxious and depressed? Do you see a beautiful young woman, or a collection of parts, each with a label: okay, too big, too small, too wide, too narrow, too short, too long, too round, too angular, flawed, imperfect, ugly?

If you're like most girls and women, you don't always feel great about what you see in the mirror. There may be parts of your body that you feel uncomfortable with or even ashamed of. Maybe you spend time trying to change parts of your body to "improve" them, or maybe you just spend time wishing that your body was different than it is.

As you know, being a teenager is not always easy. While it's certainly a time of sacred friendships and special moments, it is also a time during which you're really trying to figure out what kind of person you wish to be, which can make you uncertain and harshly self-critical.

Simone de Beauvoir wrote, "One is not born, but rather becomes, a woman." In other words, womanhood is something we learn over time, often unconsciously. Much of what we learn about womanhood we absorb as teens and young adults. During these years, we are influenced by many, many messages from a variety of sources in our lives, all of which play a role in teaching us what it means to be a young woman. Some of the most common messages young women absorb have to do with expectations about how women should look, what shape our bodies should be, and other physical attributes.

This workbook was designed to help you uncover what these messages are teaching you about being a girl and about becoming a woman. You'll examine where these messages come from and whether they've influenced your feelings about your body. Most importantly, this workbook gives you a forum to look more closely at who you are and who you want to become. And I hope that after you've spent some time with your workbook, you'll look in the mirror and see your reflection smiling back at you.

Getting Started

Before you begin your workbook, gather things that boost your creative expression—a favorite pen, markers, colored pencils, and so on. You'll also need a few fashion magazines that you don't mind cutting up, a pair of scissors, a glue stick or tape, and access to a TV.

Retreating to a comfortable spot where you can have some quiet time for yourself may allow you to clear your head and best enjoy the process of working in your book.

Remember, this is *your* workbook! That means you can do it at your own pace, whether that's all at once or a little at a time over weeks or months. You can answer the questions however you like—using words to express complete sentences, lists, or poems; through sketches, drawings, or collages of images cut from magazines and newspapers. If you have more to write or draw than space allows, feel free to use additional sheets of paper and add them to your workbook using paperclips, tape, or a stapler. Let's begin!

> **Imagination is the highest kite one can fly.**
>
> —Lauren Bacall

About You

So, Who Are You Right Now?

Let's explore a bit about how you would describe yourself right now. Let's start with one of the most basic concepts that identifies who you are: your name. Names can carry a lot of different meanings for the people to whom they are given.

Write and draw your full name in a few different creative ways (use colored pencils, markers, or crayons if you like). You can also include other names that are yours as well, like ethnic names or nicknames.

Describe how you feel about your name and what you think your name says about you. You may also explain what your name means, if you know, and whether or not you feel that the meaning relates to who you are.

Draw a picture of yourself doing an activity that is important to you or that says something about who you are (don't worry if you are not a top-notch artist, you are not being graded!).

What You Like

Take a moment to think about the following topics; then fill in the blanks describing your favorite things:

Places:

Musicians:

Holidays/Special Occasions:

Activities:

Animals:

Songs:

Names:

Foods:

Colors:

A Look in the Mirror

The People in Your Life

All the people who are part of our lives influence us in their own unique way. In other words, to know who you are, it can be helpful to consider the people who are important to you.

Friends

Write the names of a few of your closest friends in a way that illustrates their personalities. Include doodles, pictures, or words that help show what they are like.

Family

List all the people you can think of who you consider to be your family. Write three words under each person's name to describe them.

Other Important People

List some of the other people in your life who play an important role or who have an impact on you in some way. Explain who they are to you. Consider people such as your teachers, activity leaders, doctors, neighbors, coworkers (if you have a job), and others.

How do you think the following people would describe your personality?

My friends would describe me as:

My parent(s)/caregiver(s) would say I am:

My sibling(s) would say:

My most favorite teacher would describe me as:

My least favorite teacher would say:

If my pet could talk, he/she would say I am:

How would you describe yourself?

A Look in the Mirror

Our aspirations and goals in life are characteristic of our interests and desires. The next two questions will help you consider some of your own goals.

When you were a little girl and someone asked you, "What do you want to be when you grow up?," what was your answer?

What are a few "dream" jobs that you would like to have when you are an adult? Even if some of them don't seem realistic, put them down anyway.

In these past few pages, you have shared some important information about who you are. As you work through the rest of the workbook, use this section as a guide for gaining insight into yourself and what's important to you right now. Do keep in mind, your answers are likely to change over time as you grow and develop as a person. Feel free to come back to this section often and reanswer the questions, either by adding additional sheets of paper or simply thinking them over.

chapter 3

Becoming You

We are always becoming ourselves. Self-creation is a process that continuously develops and evolves as we are shaped by new experiences. Many different aspects of life influence this process: physical, spiritual, social, emotional, psychological, educational—and the list goes on.

For starters, our physical bodies are made up of a complex system of functions known as body chemistry. The basics of each person's body chemistry lie in a unique series of codes of information, called DNA, that our bodies hold within them. Each person's body chemistry, including her DNA, influences many aspects of her development.

Then there's the spiritual. Many people believe that each person has a soul or a spirit that is linked to that person's unique way of experiencing and responding to the world around her. Many believe that the essence of a person's character and personality are spiritually based.

Another primary factor that strongly influences our lifelong development as individuals is learning. What you learn and how you learn contribute tremendously to the creative process of becoming you. Much of this workbook will focus on how the things we learn shape who we are.

When we are born, our bodies are biologically set up so that we instinctively know certain things. We know to cry when we are uncomfortable, hungry, or sleepy. We know how to suckle for food. When given the opportunity, we can even recognize the smell and voice of our biological mothers.

But as newborn babies, we have a lot of learning to do. Right from the start, we begin to absorb a new world of information that will work along with our body's chemistry to help us create our maturing selves. From the moment we are born, each experience is one in which we learn something. As we grow, we continue to learn new things each day.

Read the following scenarios. Take a guess about what the characters may learn from these experiences.

While in the supermarket with her dad, 3-year-old Nyree asks for a new coloring book. Nyree's dad tells her, "Sorry Nyree, not today." Nyree begins to scream and cry, throwing herself down on the floor in the toy aisle. Nyree's Dad says, "OKAY! FINE! You can have the coloring book, just stop crying!" Nyree calms down as her dad places the coloring book in the cart and they continue with their shopping.

What might Nyree have learned from this experience?

Seventeen-year-old Rob is thrilled to have been allowed to use the family car in order to go to his high school football game. Although he is usually a very careful driver, Rob is late in picking up his friends Lisa, Young, and Brian. While on his way, Rob is pulled over by a police officer for speeding. Because Rob has never had an accident or a speeding ticket, the police officer lets him go with only a warning to slow down.

What might Rob have learned from being pulled over by the police officer.? What might he have learned as a result of *not* being issued a speeding ticket?

One afternoon while watching TV, 10-year-old Glenn and 8-year-old Mary Ellen see a commercial for a new cereal. In the commercial, there are three dancing cartoon bears, each a different color, singing a song about the cereal. Also in the commercial there is a little boy sitting in a bright, clean kitchen eating cereal with a smile on his face. In the commercial, the boy's parents come into the kitchen laughing and begin to sing along with the cartoon bears. Everyone in the commercial eats the cereal together, remarking about how delicious it is.

Draw a scene from this commercial.

What might Glenn and Mary Ellen have learned from this commercial? What do you think they might do next?

Becoming You

Bill and his younger brother Dave love to play in the snow. One winter afternoon, the boys build a snow fort. Their neighborhood friends, Craig and Jenna, join in to help out. Everyone is having a lot of fun. Just as the fort is being finished, Bill and Dave's mom and dad come out of their house. Their dad exclaims, "Wow, guys, that's a big snow fort!" Their mom says, "You all are great builders!"

What might these children have learned this afternoon? What might they do the next time it snows?

17

A Look in the Mirror

Describe an experience of your own during which you learned how to behave in a certain way through the influences in your environment:

Every experience we have teaches us something. Some of what we learn is fairly obvious, other messages are more subtle. We learn how to talk to different kinds of people in different situations. We learn how to act or behave, how to think about things, how to feel about the world, how to dress, how *not* to dress, and more. Some of what we learn has a positive effect on our lives, helping us to develop into better, happier people. But whether we realize it or not, some of what we learn negatively affects our lives, making it hard for us to grow into the kind of people we want to be.

The key to learning is being able to recognize the difference between messages that have a positive effect on our development versus those that affect us in a negative way. If we can do that, we can choose to reject messages that could harm us and accept messages that will help us develop into happier and healthier people. Some of the activities to come will help you with the tricky part: learning how to tell the difference.

chapter 4

Your Social World

So how do we learn all the things that we do? Each person learns from all the people, places, and events she encounters during her life. This world of experiences and information that surrounds a person and shapes her learning is called her *social environment*.

Your social environment includes your school; your family; your friends; your religious or spiritual group, if you have one; the television programs you watch; the music you listen to; the magazines and books you read; activity groups in which you participate; and all the other places, people, and activities that make up your life. Name some of the specific components of your social environment by filling in the missing parts of the paragraph.

My school is called:

Here is how I'd describe my school to someone who didn't know anything about it:

I watch the following TV shows regularly:

I listen to the following bands:

I am involved in the following clubs/school groups/activities:

You probably spend a good bit of time with other girls and young women around your age. You may watch some of the same shows as many of your friends, participate in the same activities, listen to some of the same music, or even live on the same street. Nevertheless, just as every person is different, every person's social environment includes some elements based on experiences that are specific to her own life

List five ways in which the social environment of your closest friend is different from yours.

1.

2.

3.

4.

5.

As you recorded on the previous page, no matter how closely connected we are to other people, aspects of everyone's social environment are unique to them alone. But everyone's social environments also have common elements throughout, and these common threads make up our larger society. In the next section, we'll explore this idea further.

chapter 5

Societal Expectations

During our lives, we receive and absorb various messages from society about what it means to be who we are. Whether or not we realize it, we learn the standards that our society holds for "acceptable" behaviors, attitudes, and ideas in all kinds of different situations. Therefore, society plays a large role in shaping the development of those who live within it, training us to fulfill certain role expectations.

Most of us hold many different roles every day of our lives. For example, in school, you are experiencing your role as "student." At home you may be "daughter" or "sister." During family gatherings, you might experience your roles of "grandchild," "cousin," or "niece." At various times, depending on who you are and what your interests are, your activities in your community might put you in the role of "athlete," "employee," or "volunteer." All of these roles allow you to express different parts of who you are.

> It is not our differences that divide us. It is our inability to recognize, accept, and celebrate those differences.
>
> —Audre Lorde

List several of the different roles you hold in your life and describe in a sentence or two what each role means to you.

1.

2.

3.

4.

5.

Select two of the roles from the previous question that you have just explored. Describe how you might behave differently when you are acting in each of them:

Why is your behavior different when you are acting in these different roles?

A Look in the Mirror

From very early in our lives, we begin to absorb some of the most significant role expectations that society has for us: expectations about what it means to be male or female. We learn which traits our society values in males and females and which traits are perceived negatively. As females, we learn what behaviors and attitudes are acceptable or unacceptable for girls and women. We also learn the "rules" about what attitudes and behaviors are acceptable and unacceptable for boys and men. Males also absorb messages about appropriate roles for men and women.

List five characteristics or traits that you have learned that females "should" possess, according to society's role expectations:

1.

2.

3.

4.

5.

Select one of the five items you just listed. Draw a picture illustrating what this characteristic means to you:

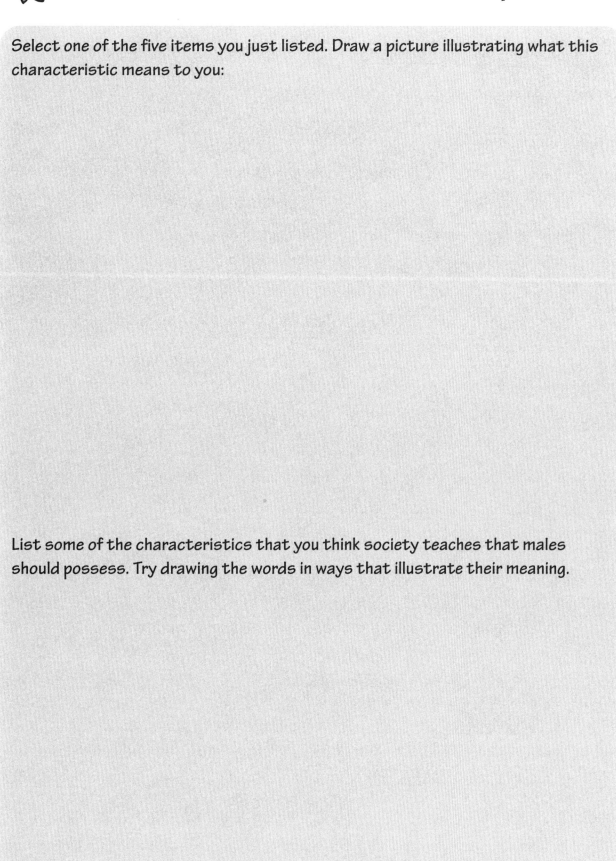

List some of the characteristics that you think society teaches that males should possess. Try drawing the words in ways that illustrate their meaning.

Listed below are some of the characteristics that American society has traditionally considered desirable in females and males.

Society's Set of Acceptable Traits

Female	Male
Caring	Strong
Compassionate	Logical
Emotional	Money-Oriented
Pretty	Distinguished
Dainty	Tough
Quiet	Athletic
Submissive	Self-Reliant
Accommodating	Fearless

Some of the traits used to label men and women may seem positive and agreeable, others may seem less so. Not all women exhibit the same kinds of characteristics. The same is true of men. Therefore, the list of traits above are *stereotypes*. In other words, they are general descriptions of, and expectations for, a group of people.

The problem with stereotypes is that they do not take into account that each of us is an individual made up of a unique set of characteristics that define who we are. Stereotypes can unfairly label and limit people. Still, the expectations outlined by our society are so powerful, and they are communicated to us so frequently, that they can influence who we become without us even realizing it. Therefore, it is important to be aware of what those expectations are.

As we have seen, within our society there exists a set of traits that are considered acceptable only for males and others only for females. So, what happens when women take on traditionally "masculine" traits, or when men exhibit traditionally "feminine" characteristics? We will explore this idea a bit further as we move on.

Circle the traits in each list below that you think are acceptable for both females and males, even if the messages given to us by our society often say otherwise:

Society's Set of Unacceptable Traits

<u>Female</u>	<u>Male</u>
Leader	Artistic
Opinionated	Sensitive
Educated	Emotional
Strong	Vegetarian
Powerful	Empathic
Ambitious	Tender
Analytical	Shy
Individualistic	Graceful
Competitive	Warm

[Society] calls an angry woman unfeminine. Because anger takes the woman out of her earth mother role as bastion of peace and calm, out of her familial role as peace-maker, out of her political role as preserver of the status quo, out of her economic role as cheap labor, out of her social role as second-class citizen. It takes her out of roles altogether and makes her a person.

—Susi Kaplow

People who do not fit into the stereotype of what our society says women and men should be are often labeled in unfair and demeaning ways. Have any of these labels ever been applied to you or someone you know?

Society's Set of Unfair Labels

Females	Males
Obnoxious	Wuss
Bitchy	Loser
Forceful	Weak
Butch	Fag
Aggressive	Childlike
Brash	Wimp
Unladylike	Dweeb
Confrontational	Overly Sensitive
Domineering	Chicken

While the first lists were made up of traits that unfairly limit males and females to certain roles, this list demonstrates how unfairly society sometimes labels people who step outside of those roles. Through labels like these, society indicates that it is wrong or bad for males and females to act in ways that are not stereotypical for their gender.

Stereotypes sometimes make us feel pressured to only express the parts of ourselves that our society considers "acceptable." This pressure stifles other characteristics that are just as important to who we are. Labels and role expectations sometimes make it difficult for us to accept and express our *true* selves. After all, none of us fits into a box. What makes each of us special is how we're different from others: the unique set of characteristics that make us who we are. These characteristics change and grow as we do.

Write down 10 characteristics you think most accurately describe your true self:

1.

2.

3.

4.

5.

6.

7.

8.

9.

10.

How many of the characteristics that you just listed seem to fit in with the list of expected traits for females?

What do you think about stereotypical traits and role expectations for males and females?

chapter 6

The Media Message

One element of our society that sends extremely powerful messages about role expectations is the *media*. The word media is used to describe widespread forms of communication such as television, magazines, advertisements, movies, books, and radio.

> The first problem for all of us, men and women, is not to learn, but to unlearn.
>
> —Gloria Steinem

List examples of your favorites in each of the categories below:

Books:

Radio Stations:

Magazines:

Movies:

Commercials:

TV Shows:

Our World in View: Exercise #1—Television

Here's an activity that will help us take a closer look at one of the most influential forms of media: TV.

View two hours worth of television programs and then answer the questions on the following pages.

Name of program(s)   Time/Day

What storylines involving women are common among the TV shows you viewed for this exercise?

What storylines involving men are common among the TV shows you viewed?

What are some of the most common activities for women characters in the TV shows?

What types of moods or attitudes do women display in the TV shows?

What characteristics would you use to describe the women who are main characters?

How do women relate to men in the storyline?

Describe the roles that women play. What jobs do they hold? What is their purpose in the plot?

What roles do men play? What jobs do they hold? What is their purpose in the plot?

What is TV telling us about what women *should* be?

In this activity, we explored how television can teach us about societal role expectations for men and women. Maybe the shows you watched fairly represented different kinds of people, or maybe the programs you watched used more stereotypes.

What was one interesting thing you noticed about how television programs represent men and women?

Our World in View: Exercise #2—Advertising

As mentioned before, another very significant force operating within the media is the advertising industry. We probably read, see, and hear more advertisements than any other form of media. They are a kind of "media within the media." For example, TV programs and radio shows are constantly interrupted by commercials. Magazines and newspapers are full of advertisements for makeup, clothing, cologne, and cigarettes.

List as many advertisements that you can remember seeing today (describe them if you can't remember what product was being advertised):

Let's take a closer look at what advertisements are *really* saying about how men and women should act.

Spend one hour surfing TV channels for commercials. Read the questions beforehand so you can answer them as you go.

Time of Day:

Day of the Week:

What ages are most of the people you see in commercials?

What race or ethnicity are most of the people you see in commercials?

How do the people featured in commercials solve their problems?

What makes the people in commercials attractive or unattractive to you?

How do the characters feel when they own or use the product being advertised?

A Look in the Mirror

When watching television advertisements, you have probably found that the people featured often seem happy, fulfilled, content, beautiful, thin, and young. Most of the people you saw in ads were probably Caucasian; most families in advertisements have a mom and a dad. In advertisements, people who are portrayed as sexy do not worry about unwanted pregnancies or sexually transmitted diseases. When people in commercials argue, are confused, or feel unfulfilled, they resolve their troubles with the right pair of shoes, snack food, or face cleanser. As Jean Kilbourne points out in her video, *Still Killing Us Softly,* "In television commercials, the most complicated problems in the world are resolved in thirty seconds just by using the right products."

Describe a commercial you have seen that shows someone fixing a problem easily because he or she had the product being advertised:

Describe a commercial you have seen that shows something incredible or amazing happening to the person in the ad because he or she had the product being advertised:

When we take a closer look at the advertising world, we find that rather than reflecting the realities of life around us, it actually involves a lot of fantasy. The truth is, in the *real* world there are all different kinds of people. People are old, young, and middle aged; they come from all over the world and from all kinds of cultures. In the real world, families are made up of all kinds of relationships: There are adoptive families and foster families, families with a mom and a dad, families with a single mom or a single dad, stepfamilies, families with two dads or families with two moms, and families headed by cousins or grandparents. And people's problems are too complicated and difficult to be solved by a brand of soda or a type of tennis shoe! In the real world, products can not make scared people feel safe or make lonely people have more friends.

So as you can see, the world we experience through advertisements and television programs is not like real life at all. Therefore, it is problematic to allow certain forms of media influence our beliefs about real life.

By now you might be thinking that even if most of the advertisements we are exposed to are set in a fantasy world, we don't really believe them. Actually, we hardly pay any attention at all to ads. Certainly, we don't let them influence what we believe about real life, right?

Write a few sentences to describe what kind of attention you pay to advertisements and what makes you think so:

While we sometimes *think* we pay very little attention to ads, it has been discovered that they have a cumulative effect on our beliefs about life. The truth is, most of us are constantly bombarded by advertising messages. When we are exposed to them frequently enough, ads actually *do* impact our learning over time because we slowly absorb their messages, sometimes not even realizing that we have. This can affect our attitudes and beliefs about the world.

1. About how many hours per day/night do you spend watching TV (be honest!)?
    _____ hours

2. About how many hours per week do you spend watching TV?
    _____ hours

3. About how many hours per week do you spend reading magazines?
    _____ hours

4. Take the two numbers you came up with from Questions 2 and 3 and add them together. What is the total?
    _____ hours

5. Take that number and multiply it by 52, filling in the result below:
    _____ hours

Circle the final number of hours that you just listed in question #5. This is the total number of hours you spend each year watching television and reading magazines.

How Do You Compare to the Average American?

According to www.tv-turnoff.org, the average American watches about 1,460 hours of television each year—that's almost 30 hours each week! Each American also spends approximately 110 hours a year reading magazines, totaling 1,570 hours of TV watching and magazine reading each year. This exposure to television and magazines alone adds up to *1,500 advertisements each day!* It has also been estimated that the average person under the age of 18 views 20,000 commercials per year. Whew! With that kind of exposure, it's easy to see how advertising could affect your perceptions over time. Being able to recognize what a large role advertising plays in our lives is the first step in discovering what we learn from all of it.

In these last few pages, we have explored some key facts that describe how much advertising and other forms of media we all absorb on a regular basis. We have also completed some activities to help us figure out what messages we might be learning through our exposure to television, commercials, and other forms of media. Now we are going to zero in on some of the specific types of media messages that have the potential to influence what we believe about femininity.

chapter 7

Women in Advertising

Despite how farfetched and silly the advertising world can sometimes seem, we are constantly tuned in to that world and its messages, and without even realizing it, we all absorb some of its elements. We may be able to laugh off certain concepts, but when we live so much of our lives with the television on, the radio blaring, and magazines strewn all around us, it's easy to lose perspective. The problem is, some of the messages we absorb can actually be quite harmful to us.

In her book *The Shelter of Each Other* (1997), psychologist and author Mary Pipher points out,

> Ads manipulate us into being dissatisfied. As businessman B.E. Puckett said, "it's our job to make people unhappy with what they have." We are encouraged to feel anxious or sorry for ourselves…advertising teaches us that people shouldn't have to suffer, that pain is unnatural and can be cured. They say that effort is bad and convenience is good and that products solve complex human problems (p. 93).

Among the most significant things that we learn from advertising are a series of messages about what it means to be a woman. Let's do our own investigation of magazine advertisements and figure out what they are *really* saying about women.

Our World in View: Exercise #3

Spend 15 or 30 minutes leafing through fashion magazines, and respond to the following questions.

List some of the products whose advertisements primarily feature women:

1.   5.

2.   6.

3.   7.

4.   8.

Describe some of the ways in which women are dressed in these ads:

What are some of the things that women are doing in these ads?

How are women portrayed in the advertisements to make the products being sold seem desirable?

List the titles of eight articles featured in the magazines you are using:

1.

2.

3.

4.

5.

6.

7.

8.

What are some of the common themes you notice among article topics?

What kinds of messages do you think fashion magazines send to their readers?

How does reading through the magazines make you feel about being you?

Societal messages about what women should be like usually focus on appearance—or, more specifically, on our bodies. And, according to these messages, being extremely thin seems to be the only acceptable standard for a woman's body size.

Although most women in today's advertisements are very thin, this is not natural for most women. As we will learn in Chapter 10, all women need a certain amount of body fat to be healthy, and our bodies fight to maintain the amount of fat they need. Therefore, very few women are able to healthily obtain the extremely thin body type that we are taught is most desirable.

Furthermore, at points in every girl's development, her body size, weight, and shape will fluctuate for biological reasons. For example, everyone experiences some type of growth spurt during puberty. During this time, our bodies grow taller and curvier. Gaining some extra weight during these years on our hips, buttocks, and breasts is a sign of normal and healthy growing. If we do not allow our bodies to gain this extra weight, we risk depriving our bodies of the extra nutrients they need to protect us from bone weakness and bone density loss.

Puberty is a very special milestone. In many cultures and religious and spiritual groups, it is considered a time for joyful rituals and celebration as a girl begins her journey into womanhood.

What is something special you could do for yourself to celebrate the years you spend growing into a woman? Is there a special adult woman that you would like to invite to participate in your celebration?

Draw a picture of a group of females of different ages having a celebration of womanhood:

Fantasy or Reality?

As we learned in Chapter 6, the world as it's portrayed through advertisements is very different from the real world. The same holds true for the women in advertisements versus "real" women we see every day. Here are a few statistics to consider:

- In the 1990s, the average model was 5'11" and weighed about 117 pounds. The average adult woman was 5'4" and 140 pounds.

- Throughout the 1990s, women were becoming 4% heavier while the average Miss Americas and *Playboy* centerfolds became 23% lighter.

- If the average store mannequin was a real woman, she would be so underweight that she would not menstruate due to her lack of sufficient body fat.

- If *Barbie* were a real woman, she would have a 39-inch bust, a 23-inch waist, and 33-inch hips. She would suffer severe back pain and have to walk on all fours due to the weight of her enormous breasts! If she somehow found a way to stand, she would not be able to walk because her feet are too tiny to support her body shape (www.mysistahs.org).

So the "ideal" women portrayed in various forms of media are nothing like most real women. In fact, most women in the advertising world are not real women at all. The truth is that, prior to a photo shoot, the women modeling for the advertisement are given a complete makeover with top-of-the-line hairstylists, wardrobe specialists, and cosmetics professionals. When taking the pictures, professional photographers often use camera angles, airbrushing, and special lighting techniques to capture the models exactly as they want them to be seen. Then, once the photographs are taken, computer specialists use high-tech equipment to alter the images. These photo retouchers have the ability to change the shape and size of a woman's thighs, waists, and arms to make her look thinner. They can smooth away wrinkles, blemishes, and skin discolorations using graphic enhancements. All it takes is the click of a mouse! The result is women who look flawless, even though no one is perfect in real life.

> Beauty deprived of its proper foils and adjuncts ceases to be enjoyed as beauty, just as light deprived of all shadows ceases to be enjoyed as light.
>
> —John Ruskin

chapter 8

Advertising: A Closer Look

So now we know that advertisements are not just harmless time-fillers between television shows or magazine articles. On the contrary, they convey messages to the people who view them; over time, those messages can influence our perceptions about womanhood and about ourselves in particular.

Miracles seem to rest, not so much upon faces or voices or healing power coming suddenly near to us from far off, but upon our perceptions being made finer so that for a moment our eyes can see and our ears can hear that which is about us always.

—Willa Cather

A Look in the Mirror

In this chapter, you'll do another magazine activity to pinpoint several types of ads featuring women and take a closer look at what they are saying. But first, let's do another drawing activity.

Draw a picture of a typical-looking female fashion model:

Our World in View: Exercise #4A

As you leaf through fashion magazines, see if you can find advertisements based on each of the following descriptions. Tear each ad out of the magazine and set it aside. Make a check in the space provided for each one you find. Once you have found all that you can, move on to Exercise #4B.*

_____ 1. Find an advertisement for any brand of make-up that features a close-up of a woman's face whom society would consider beautiful.

_____ 2. Find an ad that focuses on a specific part of a woman's body (leg, cleavage, neck) rather than the woman's whole body.

_____ 3. Find an ad that features a woman, but that pictures a man in the background who isn't fully visible (a shadow or figure)— or an ad that you think seems to imply the mistreatment of a woman, even violence against her.

_____ 4. Find an ad in which a woman seems to be in a situation that would earn her respect, independence, or a sense of freedom, but in which the reader's attention is still drawn to the woman's physical characteristics (for example, a businesswoman in a very low-cut blouse).

_____ 5. Find an ad in which an adult woman is made to look childlike or one in which a young girl or teen is dressed up in sexy clothing and wearing a lot of makeup.

_____ 6. Find an ad in which a woman seems to be competing with other women, is against other women, or feels threatened by them in some way.

_____ 7. Find an ad with a woman in a very seductive pose, caressing herself suggestively, or one in which a woman is barely dressed.

_____ 8. Find an ad with a positive message for women. For example, the ad could feature a woman who is of a larger size, or it could focus in a respectful way on a woman's important accomplishment.

---

* Many of the concepts that this exercise addresses are extrapolated from Dr. Jean Kilbourne's 1979 video, *Still Killing Us Softly* (Cambridge, MA: Cambridge Documentary Films, Inc.).

Our World in View: Exercise #4B

Refer back to the ads you selected in Exercise #4A while reading the corresponding explanations on the following pages. On each page, glue or tape down the ad you found that matches the numbered descriptions (feel free to trim the ads down or fold them for a better fit).

1.   Most cosmetic ads display an image of what our society considers "perfect" beauty. The problem is that we cannot help but fail to live up to this standard of perfection. These women are not real. Their photographs are often airbrushed and computerized to make them look flawless. The women have few or no wrinkles, no blemishes, no stray hairs, probably not even a freckle! Real women are not perfect. Our "flaws" are actually special traits that make each of us a unique human being.

2. Some companies only focus on a particular body part of a woman in their advertisements. By picking apart our bodies, these ads reduce the value of a woman from a whole person to a piece of something that people desire—all to entice the reader to purchase the product being advertised. This technique allows people to think of a woman as less than a human being and as just a body part. Dehumanizing a person is dangerous, because it is often the first step in being able to justify acting violently against them.

3. Ads displaying women interested in lurking mystery men send the message that a shadowy male figure could indicate the beginning of a sensual romance. In reality, most women would probably be frightened, not aroused, if a man approached them in such a manner. Some ads go as far as depicting blatantly violent scenes involving women. Whether the violence is actually displayed or just suggested, this is an attempt to make a frightening and dangerous reality seem surreal, glamorous, and alluring, and to present women as passive, submissive, and dependent on men and their whims. The message presented in ads such as these contributes to a tone of violence against women in our society.

4. Ads in which women are pictured as accomplished or powerful sometimes have messages that actually mock women or their achievements, making them seem much less important. Many ads featuring businesswomen actually focus on the woman's pantyhose or cleavage rather then taking seriously her role as strong or independent woman.

5. The qualities of innocence and naiveté have become sexualized in American culture. Ads that present sensual adult women as childlike, or ads where children or teens are made to look like sexually appealing adults, create a climate in which children are viewed as sexual objects. In a society where the sexual abuse of children and teens is becoming more and more common, this is extremely dangerous.

6. Because women try to achieve a standard of beauty that is impossible, we feel like we are always competing with each other. It is almost as if we have to be at war, resenting women we perceive as beautiful and worrying that they are a threat to us and our relationships. Unfortunately, this often keeps us from addressing the real problem as a team.

7. Lots of ads portray women in seductive poses or in various states of undress. Ads like these offer the impression that women are interested in fulfilling the sexual fantasies of men anytime and anywhere. It sends the message to women and men that women exist to meet the sexual desires of boys and men. Furthermore, such ads teach girls that their greatest worth is in their sexuality, rather then in the other qualities that make them unique individuals. Certainly, all people have sexual feelings; however, there is much more to all of us than that!

8. Several companies have begun to demonstrate a much higher level of respect for women by genuinely acknowledging their accomplishments and strengths. Other companies have begun to use models of average or larger sizes, or even make fun of the unrealistic expectations placed upon women. Although there are many destructive advertisements today, many women are making their voices heard against these messages. As a result, there is hope for a more positive future for women.

Ads do sell products, but they also sell a great deal more. They sell values, they sell images, they sell concepts of love, sexuality, romance, success, popularity, and perhaps most important, of normalcy. To a very great extent they tell us who we are and who we should be.

Now that you know some more about advertisements and what they are saying, let's move on and explore how this can affect our beliefs about ourselves.

chapter 9

Your Self-Image

As we learned before, advertising has a cumulative effect on our beliefs. Therefore, advertisements and television programs that focus primarily on a women's appearance teach their viewers to do the same. In such an environment, it's easy to believe that your appearance is your most important quality.

> Beauty is not in the face;
> beauty is a light in the heart.
>
> —Khalil Gibran

List the three women whom you would like to be for a day. Then explain in a few sentences why it would be a great experience to be them.

Woman #1: _____

I would like to be her for a day because:

Woman #2: _____

I would like to be her for a day because:

Woman #3: _____

I would like to be her for a day because:

Ask yourself the following questions about the previous activity:

Did I select most of the women based on physical characteristics (the way they look, how thin or sexy they are)? Explain your answer.

Was I able to list positive traits that the women possess based on their personalities and nonphysical characteristics? Explain your answer.

A Look in the Mirror ──────────────

In Chapter 15, we'll explore some characteristics and qualities that *truly* make a woman worthy of admiration!

Now that we have a better understanding about the kinds of messages we absorb from elements of our social environments, let's explore how this affects the way we view ourselves.

How I feel about my body in general:

My favorite part(s) of my body and why it's my favorite:

The part(s) of my body I would most like to change:

Some things girls do to try to look the way they think they ought to:

List five ways girls are negatively affected by the messages they receive from society about what a woman *should* be:

1.

2.

3.

4.

5.

As we are learning, society places a great deal of pressure on women to fit into a mold of certain characteristics and attributes. These messages impact the way we feel about ourselves and our bodies. Once we uncover what we are being taught, however, we can figure out which messages help us feel good about ourselves and which do not. Then we can decide which kind of learning we want to accept into our lives and which kind we want to reject.

chapter 10

Straight Talk About Dieting

Through media images in magazines and TV shows, we are taught that being thin will make us well-liked, successful, and happy. Being constantly bombarded by the images of fantasy women we see in advertising, it's easy to begin to believe that to be happy, accepted, loved, and self-confident, we have to look like them. These misleading messages push many women to constantly battle with their bodies through dieting and over-exercising. For most healthy women, however, achieving this image of womanhood is unrealistic to virtually impossible, since such images of "perfection" are not based on real life. This "ideal body" also does not take into account some of the natural and healthy developmental changes that women experience throughout their lives.

Nevertheless, some women do pretty dramatic things to be thin. Many popular actresses and models have to do dangerous and exhausting things to their bodies to look the way they do. Some of them have begun to speak out very honestly about their struggles to help other women avoid some of the pressures and problems they have experienced.

> **It is not easy to find happiness in ourselves, and it is not possible to find it elsewhere.**
>
> —Agnes Repplier

List three famous women who you think look extremely thin:

1.

2.

3.

As a result of this push to be thin, weight loss programs and products have become extremely popular in the United States. Everywhere we look we see books on dieting, exercise videos, advertisements for diet programs, and all kinds of pills and shakes claiming they can "help us" lose weight. As women, we are made to feel so bad about our bodies that we spend an enormous amount of time, energy, and money trying to "improve" ourselves.

List and briefly describe the first five dieting products or programs you think of:

1.

2.

3.

4.

5.

Unfortunately, these programs prey on our feelings of insecurity and disdain toward our bodies. The dieting industry benefits tremendously from our feelings of inadequacy, making billions of dollars each year in North America alone!

While some of these products and programs may be temporarily helpful, many of them will not help us lose real weight for the long term, as you will read about in this chapter.

Describe some of the diets you have tried or someone you know has tried:

Were the dieting goals met? If they were met, for how long were they sustained?

The problem with dieting to lose weight is that diets do not really work. Sure, some weight-loss programs focus on healthy eating and exercise and therefore can help people achieve and maintain a healthy weight. Most diets, however, focus on other types of weight loss using special products or plans that involve depriving your body of the calories or food components it needs to function normally. Some diets even involve introducing substances into the body such as special pills, powders, or drinks. These diets do *not* make you thin. People only think dieting works because the whole idea of dieting is based on commonly held beliefs that are actually untrue! These myths harm those who diet and eventually lead to failure. Sometimes they also lead to unhealthy and dangerous eating behaviors. In reality, you cannot lose real weight and keep it off over the long term by dieting.

Dangerous Dieting Myths

Body fat is the enemy.

Most people have been taught that body fat is bad and unhealthy. The truth is that not all body fat is bad and healthy bodies can come in all sizes! In fact, a certain amount of body fat is *healthy* for us and is necessary for our survival. Girls need to store certain amounts of fat to achieve puberty. Women's bodies naturally do the same to support their ability to have children and breastfeed, even if they choose not to actually have children. This particular fat is stored in our hips, thighs, and buttocks. It is resistant to weight loss. Our body's resistance to losing this fat is its way of trying to keep us at a healthy weight. Furthermore, fat is a protective tissue that shields our muscles, tendons, and bones from impact and damage. Women who have little or no body fat risk suffering more frequent injuries and having more brittle bones than other women.

Dieting makes you thin.

The reason most people diet is because they think it will make them thinner. People who diet the most actually end up weighing *more* than the average woman who does not frequently diet. Why? Some doctors and scientists believe in something called the "set point theory." This theory argues that each person's metabolism (the rate at which their body burns up calories from food) adjusts itself to maintain a comfortable weight. When we restrict our calorie intake through dieting, our metabolism slows down. This is nature's way of keeping us from starving. Under dieting conditions, our bodies are biologically conditioned to *fight* weight loss by slowing down our body's ability to burn up our food! So, the more we diet, the more fat our body stores and the slower we burn calories. People who regularly diet can really interfere with their body's ability to use calories for everyday functioning.

Another reason that dieters usually weigh more then the average person is that dieting can encourage bingeing. Bingeing happens when our bodies are so deprived that we feel the uncontrollable desire to eat a lot of food all at once. This is our body's way of getting the nourishment it needs when we have been depriving ourselves, and of storing extra calories to maintain our health.

If your diet fails, you are the failure.

Most of us feel very guilty if we do not end up losing the weight we had hoped to when dieting. We blame ourselves for not working hard enough or having enough willpower to resist eating what our body craves. In actuality, the dieting industry is misleading us when they make it seem as though a diet will work if we just do it right. This way, if the diet works temporarily, the program gets the credit. When our bodies begin fighting us harder to maintain the fat they need, the diet begins to fail. Then the dieting industry blames the dieter by sending the message that the dieter must not have followed the program properly. After all, their diet sure seemed to have worked for those super-thin actors and actresses in the diet commercials, right?

Fat is ugly.

Most of us have been trained to think that the only beautiful women's bodies are thin ones. But throughout history, thinness in women has almost never been sought after until now. Up through the 1950s, attractiveness was largely related to physical attributes associated with a woman's fertility, which meant that wide hips, a full bust, and a large bottom were most idolized. In contrast, thinness was associated with poverty, low social status, and infertility (women who do not have enough body fat often do not menstruate regularly and therefore have difficulty conceiving children). Sadly, during these years, *thin* women were made to feel insecure about being less full-figured. Many filled out their figures with fake thigh, buttock, and calf inserts to make their bodies look more shapely and voluptuous. During the early 1900s, America's favorite female stars were much heavier. With their natural feminine curves and round-ness, they were considered sexy, beautiful, and healthy.

So what caused this huge change in our thinking about weight? Historically, it was considered a sign of wealth to be full figured. Wealthy people had plenty to eat, making plumpness a sign of status. On the other hand, the poor often had little to eat and had to do physical labor, leaving them much skinnier then the rich. By the late 1950s the world was moving at a faster pace, and wealthy people began spending their leisure time doing more physical activities. When the wealthy began to slim down, this new body type became the sign of social status. The pressure to be thin took hold quickly in American society. This change created even greater pressure, as having easy access to unhealthy, high-calorie foods became the norm, as did limited time for exercise and staying fit. This combination has led people to have great admiration for what is most difficult to achieve: a slender body! Nowadays, because we have been trained from childhood to associate slenderness with attractiveness, we continue to buy into the image of extreme thinness as the only acceptable body. The truth is that, fat or thin, all different shapes, sizes, and types of women's bodies can be beautiful!

In American society, thinness for women is equated with happiness, fulfillment, and desirability. This fact, combined with myths about dieting and body size, leads many women to diet, drastically reducing their caloric intake, thinking that this will make them thin. Not only *do* diets *not* make you thin, they also cannot make you happier, more fulfilled, more loved, or more desirable. Diets *can* lead to feelings of anxiety and depression, however. Let's move on and see how. Then we will explore how to truly be healthy without dieting.

Drastic Measures: Eating Disorders

Life poses challenges, difficulties, and struggles for everyone. It can be scary when big changes take place, when we are unhappy, or when something traumatic happens to you or someone you care for. Life also holds opportunities for great joy and moments of calm and ease. Everyone experiences times when we feel more vulnerable and other times when we feel stronger and more self-confident.

While we all have ups and downs in life, for some, painful experiences are more prevalent. For example, some of us feel as though we have to be perfect in order to be loved. Others of us live in an environment where we are not allowed the opportunity to make choices for ourselves. Some of us have been hurt or mistreated in various ways, making us feel out of control and unsafe. Many people have feelings of insecurity, and some people are deeply sensitive. All of these circumstances can lead to emotional pain.

When a person experiences emotional pain, it's natural for her to try to find a way to alleviate those difficult feelings. There are healthy and unhealthy ways of doing this. Unfortunately, not everyone has learned or been taught healthy ways to manage and express painful emotions. Those of us without the tools to cope with our feelings in a positive way may turn instead to unhealthy means in an effort to make ourselves feel soothed and more in control of our lives.

As you know, one of the greatest societal pressures placed upon young women today is that of achieving a very slim figure. Partly because of this, some girls and women turn to weight loss in order to achieve a greater sense of control in uncertain times. This tactic can quickly lead to drastic measures that endanger their physical health and further threaten their emotional health.

Women have been doing drastic things to their bodies to meet the changing expectations of society for many years. In the late nineteenth and early twentieth centuries, for example, many women wore corsets. This type of undergarment was pulled tight around a woman's waist to make it look smaller while her hips and bust remained full. Corsets were tied so tightly that women would sometimes faint from the lack of oxygen traveling through their blood and into their brain. Women who wore corsets regularly over long periods of time actually suffered physical problems as the corset began changing the shape of their ribcage so that filling their lungs to capacity when breathing was near impossible.

Today's drastic attempts at thinness are still unhealthy and can lead to an increased risk for the development of life-threatening illnesses called eating disorders.

Have you heard the term "eating disorder" before now?

Can you name an eating disorder?

Write what you know about eating disorders. If you have not yet learned about eating disorders, write what you imagine they may involve:

Let's explore the danger signs and medical consequences of three eating disorders so you can begin to recognize them if they are present in your friends, your family members, or yourself. In Chapter 12 we will explore how to get help for someone whom you believe is suffering from an eating disorder.

Anorexia Nervosa

Anorexia nervosa, commonly called anorexia, is an eating disorder involving a person's preoccupation with dieting and thinness. People with anorexia have an intense fear of fat and are very focused on food and weight. As we just learned, people with anorexia are often struggling with issues of control and safety. So while a woman might try to feel more in control by strictly monitoring what she eats, she could actually end up taking it to an extreme, making herself ill. In the end, people with anorexia are much more out of control when it comes to their health and their lives than they ever were before.

Warning Signs of Anorexia

- Significant weight loss
- Intense fear of weight gain
- Feeling fat even after losing weight
- Continued dieting even when thin
- Lying about eating
- Preferring to eat alone
- Anxiety, depression
- Exercising compulsively
- Loss of menstrual period
- Constipation
- Periods of hyperactivity

- Dry, brittle skin
- Shortness of breath
- Cold hands and feet
- Heart tremors
- Weakness, exhaustion
- Fainting
- Hair loss
- Growth of fine body hair on arms and legs (called "lanugo," this is the body's attempt to warm itself since the body fat has decreased or gone)

Medical Consequences of Anorexia

People with anorexia are at risk of developing serious medical problems that could ultimately cause death. These include:

Shrunken organs

Low blood pressure

Slowed metabolism and reflexes

Irregular heartbeat

Bone mineral loss

Osteoporosis

Low body temperature

Cardiac arrest

Liver failure

Kidney failure

Start a revolution: Stop hating your body.

—Anonymous

Bulimia Nervosa

Another common eating disorder is bulimia nervosa. Bulimia involves frequent episodes of binge eating (quickly eating a very large amount of food in one sitting), usually followed by purging. Purging means ridding the body of the food by throwing up, using laxatives, or exercising compulsively. After the bingeing and purging cycle, people with bulimia usually feel guilty and ashamed. People with bulimia are usually of average weight or even slightly overweight. As with anorexia, this disease is often triggered by a person's need to cope with a deeper problem.

Warning Signs of Bulimia

- Bingeing or eating uncontrollably
- Purging
- Bloodshot eyes
- Using bathroom frequently after meals
- Heartburn/bloating
- Depression
- Irregular periods
- Dry or withered skin around the fingers
- Feeling out of control

- Dental problems, tooth decay
- Mood swings
- Constipation
- Weakness, exhaustion
- Indigestion
- Dehydration
- Sore throat
- Swollen glands in neck and face
- Vomiting blood

Medical Consequences of Bulimia

As with anorexia, serious medical consequences are associated with bulimia, including:

An imbalance of nutrients in the body

Irregular heartbeat

Damage to bowels, liver, kidneys, esophagus, and throat

Cardiac arrest

Binge Eating

Binge eating is a third common eating disorder. It involves compulsive overeating, which is usually done in private and kept secret. People with this disorder frequently binge but do not purge. Binges are usually followed by feelings of intense guilt and shame. Once again, food is used as a means of coping with psychological problems and difficult emotions. Depression is common among people with a binge eating disorder.

Warning Signs of Binge Eating

- Eating when not physically hungry
- Antisocial behavior
- Feeling unable to stop eating voluntarily
- Frequent dieting
- Feeling ashamed

- Weight fluctuations
- Depressed mood
- Obesity
- Awareness that eating patterns are not normal

Medical Consequences of Binge Eating

Binge eating is associated with its own set of medical problems, including:

High blood pressure

High cholesterol

Gall bladder disease

Diabetes

Heart disease

Certain types of cancer

Many women experience some of the danger signs of eating disorders at some point in their lives. Identifying one or even a few of these signs does not necessarily mean that the person has an eating disorder. When many symptoms are linked together, however, these symptoms can indicate that a person is developing a serious problem or that one already exists. If someone you know (including yourself!) is doing unhealthy things to her body, it is important that that she get help and talk with an adult about her concerns. The next chapter contains more information about how to seek help for yourself or someone you know.

Is there someone in your life who you think may have an eating disorder?

Describe the attitudes or behaviors of which you are aware that lead you to think it could be an eating disorder.

Clearly, when we engage in these behaviors, we are not "rewarded" with a desirable body type. Instead we find ourselves dealing with pain, struggle, and serious medical problems. Tragically, between 5% and 20% of people who suffer from an eating disorder die as a result of the harm they have done to their bodies. Others afflicted with eating disorders experience a constant battle with eating and a continual preoccupation with food and weight. For some, this struggle takes a lifetime to overcome. Luckily, many people who are able to get the help they need to address their eating disorder can go on to live a healthy life! Getting well does require that the person afflicted with the disorder really wants to get well, and that she has ongoing professional treatment and monitoring as well as strong emotional support from the people in her life.

Getting Help

Most people are unsure about how to get help for a person who has eating problems or bad feelings about her body. If you suspect that someone you care about is in trouble, however, it's important to take action. These issues can be very serious and you should not try to manage them on your own. Start by voicing your concerns to the person you're concerned about and encouraging her to talk with an adult she trusts. If she is not receptive to your concerns, talk with an adult *you* trust.

People who are specially trained to help others overcome difficult mental health issues are usually called counselors. Counselors can include social workers, psychologists, licensed therapists, and psychiatrists. They may work in schools, in doctor's offices, in after-school programs, in offices out of their homes, in hospitals, and many other places. This group of professionals can offer help for all kinds of problems such as problems with relationships, depression, anxiety or stress, friends, school, and problems with eating, including bad feelings about ourselves or our bodies. Counselors use a variety of techniques to help the people with whom they work, such as talking together about the problems and doing special activities and assignments—even playing certain kinds of games can be therapeutic.

What do you think about counselors and people who see them?

Some people are uncomfortable or embarrassed about the idea of meeting with a counselor. They may be afraid to share private information with someone they do not know, or they may think that asking for help means that they are too weak to help themselves. The truth is, because we are human, we all have troubles in our lives at one time or another. None of us is perfect. Counselors work with all different kinds of people needing guidance, assistance, and support. Seeking the help of others shows that not only do you care about yourself, but you also have the courage required to access the support and services you need to be healthy. Good counselors will do their very best to make the people who meet with them feel comfortable and secure to share their problems at their own pace.

The key to having a successful counseling experience is finding the right counselor. It is a good idea to get a recommendation from someone you know or from your local mental health community rather then trying to find a counselor through the phone book. In addition, asking potential counselors some initial questions before you begin counseling can help you decide whether they are well equipped to deal with the issues that concern you.

Below are five suggested questions to ask when speaking with potential counselors about body image issues:

1. What is your professional experience with eating disorders and body image issues?

2. What are your values and beliefs about heavy women?

3. Will you be able to provide me with suggestions at each session that will help me achieve my counseling goals?

4. What is your understanding of the role that culture and media play in the lives of women?

5. Will you be able to identify my strengths and help me build on them?

After meeting with a counselor for a session or two, you will probably get a sense of his or her counseling style. A counselor should be caring, empathic, and encouraging. She or he should help you develop feelings of strength and hope. Most importantly, when searching for the right counselor, listen to your instincts. If it seems as though the services provided by your current counselor are not helping you, consider asking for a referral to another counselor in order to find a better match for your needs.

> I have come to believe over and over again that what is most important to me must be spoken, made verbal, and shared, even at the risk of having it bruised or misunderstood. That the speaking profits me, beyond any other effect.
>
> —Audre Lorde

What are some of the issues in your life that are most troubling to you?

Are any of your current problems or difficulties very hard for you to manage on your own right now?

Who are the people in your life that you trust the most?

Are you able to talk with the people you trust about things in your life that trouble you? Have they been helpful to you?

Have you, or has anyone you know, ever met with a counselor? What were the circumstances?

What do you think it would be like (or what was it like) to talk with a counselor about issues that concern you?

If you decided you would like to meet with a counselor to get some extra help dealing with a difficult problem, what might be your first step?

chapter 13

Healthy Living, Not Dead-End Dieting

Healthy Eating

Now that we know that dieting is not a good way to maintain our health or keep off extra weight in the long term, in this section, we'll look at what our body does need to be healthy, lean, and fit.

One main component of a healthy lifestyle involves eating properly, as we have to eat in order to live. In his book, *Eating Well for Optimum Health* (2000), Dr. Andrew Weil explains:

> The body requires energy for all of its functions, from the beating of the heart and the elimination of wastes to the transmission of electrical and chemical signals in the nervous system. It gets its energy from food, by taking it in, digesting it, and metabolizing its components. Food is fuel that contains energy from the sun, originally captured and stored by green plants, then passed along to fruits, seeds, and animals. Humans eat these foods, and burn the fuel they contain—that is, combine it with oxygen in a controlled fashion to release and capture the stored solar energy. As long as we live, we have to eat and eat often (p. 9).

Diagram the movement of the energy from the sun into food that we then use as fuel for our bodies:

Today there are many different philosophies about nutrition and healthy eating. All the information available on this topic can be confusing. But there *is* a difference between a healthy regimen, even a nontraditional one, and unhealthy or harmful eating.

Healthy eating involves some standard principles that diets do not:

- Healthy eating means we choose foods that are nutritionally beneficial to our bodies, but we are not so rigid that we deny ourselves foods we like. Healthy eating allows us to enjoy treats from time to time, as long as we use some restraint.

- Healthy eating does not require a daily meal plan. It does involve monitoring what we eat on a regular basis to make sure we are eating some of all the types of food that we need to be healthy.

- Healthy eating means eating when we are physically hungry and stopping when our physical hunger is satisfied. Sometimes people confuse emotions such as loneliness, anxiety, sadness, and anger with feelings of physical hunger. It is important to learn to recognize the difference between physical and emotional hunger so that when we are feeling emotionally needy, we can cope with these feelings in healthier ways then overeating.

- Healthy eating can include three meals a day or involve munching on smaller, more frequent meals throughout the day. It is flexible and varies in response to our hunger.

Which of the above ideas do you think sounds easiest to follow?

Which of the above ideas do you think sounds hardest to follow?

Now that we have reviewed some of the principles of healthy eating, let's examine some specifics:

For many years, just about anyone concerned with healthy eating relied on the traditional food pyramid guide. Created by the United States Department of Agriculture, it outlines different food groups and daily serving guidelines. You have probably learned about the food pyramid in a nutrition or science class at school. Many believe it is the best model on which to base your eating regimen.

The food pyramid guide suggests that we eat 6 to 11 servings of foods from the grain group—that is, breads, cereals, rice, and pastas—each day. Although this may sound like a lot, a serving of pasta is a lot less then we would think: One serving of pasta is about the size of your fist, and a slice of bread would also be considered a serving. The food pyramid guide also suggests two to four servings per day of fruit and three to five servings of vegetables. The pyramid recommends we eat two to three servings per day from the dairy group (milk, yogurt, cheese) and two to three from the protein group (meat, poultry, fish, dry beans, eggs, and nuts). At the top of the pyramid are fats, oils, and sweets, which the guide recommends we consume sparingly (USDA, 1996).

List your favorite foods from the following groups. (If you prefer, you may draw them instead, or cut and paste pictures of them from magazines.)

The grain group:

The fruit group:

The vegetable group:

The dairy group:

The protein group:

Fats or sweets:

While the food pyramid is a popular philosophy of healthy eating, many types of healthy eating models exist. What is most important to consider is that all bodies need certain food components, each of which play an important role in our ability to function.

According to Dr. Weil, one way to categorize the essential food components is to include categories of food like "macronutrients," "micronutrients," and water. Macronutrients include carbohydrates, fats, and protein, while micronutrients comprise vitamins, minerals, fiber, and protective phytochemicals.

Carbohydrates break down in our bodies into simple sugar glucose, which is used for energy. Carbohydrates also contain valuable amounts of other nutrients. Carbohydrate foods include bread, cereals, pasta, rice, grains, and potatoes, as well as fruits and some vegetables. An important consideration in selecting good sources of carbohydrates is a measurement called the "Glycemic Index" or GI. This measurement determines how quickly various starchy foods impact our levels of blood sugar. The GI then affects your general health, your tendency for weight gain, and your energy level. Foods with a higher GI rating create a surge in your blood sugar that strains your system and is followed by a sharp decrease in your energy. Carbohydrates with a low or moderate GI rating are better for your blood sugar levels then those with a higher rating. Some of the better carbohydrate choices include brown or long grain white rice, whole wheat bread, pasta cooked "al dente" (slightly firm), carrots, peas, sweet potatoes and yams, most fruits, peanuts, and popcorn.

Fats are also used as a source of energy. As we learned previously, the body needs fats to grow and to repair tissue, and fat is also a protective tissue that shields our bones and muscles from injury. Fats are classified as either saturated or unsaturated. Saturated fats are found mainly in foods of animal origin such as fatty meats, butter, full-fat milks, cheese, and some vegetable oils. It's better for you to eat fewer saturated fats, as they can increase your blood cholesterol level, which is unhealthy for your heart. Unsaturated fats are found in olive oil, some leaner meats, some dairy products, sunflower oils, fish oils, eggs, soybeans, nuts, seeds, avocados, and olives. In moderate quantities, these kinds of fats are healthier for our bodies than saturated fats.

Protein is an essential part of all the cells in our bodies, especially our muscles and skin. It enables our bodies to grow and repair tissue, and it supplies crucial amino acids and enzymes. An important consideration in your protein intake relates to how your body burns protein as fuel. The energy burned from carbohydrates and fats is "clean" fuel, but protein is not a "clean-burning" fuel. As it is burned, it leaves behind ammonia, which is toxic to the human body. Thankfully, the body perceives this ammonia as waste and eliminates it through urination or bowel movements. If you eat too much protein, however, you risk overworking the organs in your body that eliminate waste. Foods that have adequate protein include grains, soybeans, nuts, fish, beans, some dairy products, and meats.

Vitamins are chemicals, most of which can only be obtained from food or pill supplements. Those who eat a variety of fresh fruits and vegetables, grains, dairy products, fish, and meat generally get enough vitamins. If you eat additional fresh fruits and vegetables, your diet may provide enough vitamins A, C, and E to help prevent osteoporosis and possibly some forms of cancer.

Minerals are also necessary for a healthy eating regimen. Your body needs at least 20 minerals: iron, calcium, iodine, chromium, potassium, selenium, zinc, and sodium (salt) are some of the more common ones. Iron and calcium are sometimes added to foods such as bread and orange juice to help people get more minerals in their diet. A well-balanced eating regimen usually provides enough iron, calcium, and iodine. Many people eat too much sodium, however, and this is known to increase the risk of heart disease for people who already have high blood pressure.

Fiber is a big contributor to your overall health. Fiber helps with digestion and other related body functions by helping food move through your system and making the waste pass out of your system more easily. Foods with a lot of fiber include spinach, apples, whole wheat bread, rice, oats, rye, barley, and kidney beans.

Protective phytochemicals and their role in healthy eating have only recently begun to be more thoroughly researched. We now know that these chemicals help build up the body's defenses against many harmful diseases, including cancer. While phytochemicals are not thought to be essential to a healthy diet, they play a significant role in helping us combat toxins and pollutants in the environment. Plants and vitamins that contain various types of phytochemicals include the darker colored fruits and vegetables, like berries, red grapes, red cabbage, and dark leafy greens. Phytochemicals are also stored in orange fruits (peaches, mangos, cantaloupes, carrots, pumpkin, squash, sweet potato), soy products, garlic, ginger, and some varieties of mushrooms.

Water makes up about 65% to 70% of our bodies. We lose approximately $3\frac{1}{2}$ pints of water every day just from exhaling, sweating, and urinating. Most foods are about 70% water. Many nutritionists recommend that we drink 64 ounces of water each day—about eight glasses.

A Look in the Mirror

Briefly describe your general eating habits by filling in the following:

I eat the following foods on a regular basis:

Typically I eat _____ (small, medium, large, extra-large) size meals _____ times per day.

I find that I eat the most when:

I eat the least when:

My family eats together _____ times per week.

My favorite restaurants are:

Three things I'd like to change about the way I eat are:

1.

2.

3.

So now we know that the food we eat is crucial to ensuring our physical health. We will only get out of our food what the foods we choose have to provide to our bodies. So the next time you sit down for a meal, consider the old saying, "You are what you eat!"

Active Living

Along with healthy eating, it's vital to keep our bodies moving. Just as with eating philosophies, there are many philosophies about healthy exercise. These principles, however, are consistently thought to be true about exercise.

- Regular exercise at a moderate rate is better for the heart and bones than sporadic high-intensity work.

- Exercise done on a regular basis can help people cope better with stress, anxiety, and sadness by releasing certain chemicals and hormones in our bodies.

- Physical activity should involve something you like to do so that you will keep doing it. It can include walking the dog, gardening, swimming, dancing, skiing, tennis, yoga, bowling, biking, hiking, jumping rope, in-line skating, aerobics, kickboxing, jumping on a trampoline, and lots of other enjoyable activities.

- Exercise should be dependent on age, health, and other factors. Ask your doctor about exercise that's right for you.

List some other important factors of healthy exercise that you have learned over the years:

List some of your favorite physical activities, or draw a picture of a group of people doing some of these activities:

Describe the type and amount of exercise you currently get per week:

How could you learn more about nutrition and exercise?

Please remember, if you have specific medical needs or if you have questions, talk to your doctor before beginning any kind of exercise routine or eating change.

A Healthy Body Image

Everyone has positive and negative feelings about aspects of themselves at different times in their lives—or even on different days of the week! Sometimes, feeling unhappy with a certain aspect of yourself can encourage you to work toward being an even better person. But sometimes it can make you feel bad and discourage you from taking good care of yourself.

The term *body image* is used to describe the way we perceive our bodies and how we feel about them. A healthy body image is present when a person's mental picture of her body is accurate, and her feelings, assessment, and relationship toward her body are positive, confident, and self-caring. The major components of healthy body image include:

- Demonstrating care for the body through the use of good hygiene, healthy eating, and exercising.

- Having a positive self-concept and the ability to make positive judgments about yourself.

- Finding outlets for self-expression, which may include writing, painting, music, dance, and the ability to talk about your feelings.

- Developing confidence in your physical abilities.

- Developing a positive self-awareness, value for yourself and resistance to negative messages.

To develop a positive or healthy body image, it is important to first recognize what kind of body image you have right now. Ways to judge your current body image include paying attention to how you care for yourself as well as noticing what you say or think about yourself each day. Let's explore a bit about your body image as it stands today by completing the activities ahead.

Draw a picture of the way your body looks right now (you can do an outline of a shape or a more detailed illustration):

If different from your previous drawing, draw a picture of how you would *like* your body to look:

Describe the way you feel about your body right now:

I exercise _____ times per week.

Usually I get exercise by doing the following activities:

I weigh myself approximately _____ times per month.

When I get dressed for school, I usually try on _____ different outfits before finding something to wear.

Here are some things I do, say, or think that let me know that I have some positive feelings about my body:

Here are some things I do, say, or think that let me know that I have some negative feelings about my body:

When you think of words like "positive" or "confident," what other words or images come to mind? (Write or draw your response.)

Describe what you think "self-caring" means (Write or draw your response.):

The most important factor in achieving a healthy body image is accepting and loving your body, no matter what kind of body you have!

Promoting a Healthy Body Image

1. **Challenge yourself to be more aware of some of the harmful messages you receive through your social environment,** including the types of media we examined in earlier chapters. Pay close attention to commercials, billboards, bumper stickers, people's comments, and all other messages that make you feel badly about yourself, and make a conscious effort to reject negative messages. Consider fighting against companies who promote negative messages through letter writing or other nonviolent forms of protest.

2. **Write a list of some of your favorite things about yourself that are not related to how you look or your weight.** Post the list on a mirror to use it as a reminder of some of your wonderful and important qualities. Add to the list as you discover new things that make you proud to be you!

3. **Spend time with people in your life who have a positive influence on you and make you feel good about yourself.** It is a lot easier to be accepting and loving toward yourself when you are surrounded by others who know how wonderful you are and who can be supportive of your most important attributes.

4. **Reflect on all the wonderful things your body does for you!** Our bodies are designed to take us to great places and allow us to explore all that life has to offer. Physically, our bodies are amazing machines! The human body has a powerful ability to promote its own healing when we are sick or injured. It is able to turn the food we eat into energy. The body knows how to rid itself of waste material that is unneeded or harmful to us. It even uses certain organs to clean the rest of our system and keep it functioning at its best. And of course, your body enables you to do fabulous things such as dance, sing, run, and laugh! All of that is pretty incredible, don't you think?

5. **Focus on yourself as a whole person rather than a collection of body parts that you either like or dislike.** Our bodies are not bags of parts to be picked over by our minds! We should all be accepted and appreciated as entire beings—by ourselves and by others.

6. **Put a stop to negative thoughts about the appearance of your body.** These criticisms do not help you become a better and happier you; they only contribute to negative self-image. When you catch yourself saying bad things about your body, instead substitute a positive statement that will make you feel better.

7. **Do nice things for yourself and for your body.** Select clothes that make you feel comfortable and content with your body rather then forcing yourself into outfits that make you feel dissatisfied with yourself. Take time for a

bubble bath or give yourself a foot massage as a way of appreciating your body. Honor your body's need for rest and rejuvenation by taking naps when you feel the need, creating a peaceful place for quiet or solitude, and enjoying outlets of creative expression (www.nationaleatingdisorders.org).

Most importantly, in your quest for a healthy body image, it is crucial to remember that your body is *not* the most important thing about you! Regardless of the kind of pressure you may feel in regard to your body size—whether it is to be thin, to have larger breasts, or to be "curvier" and more voluptuous—the bottom line is that it is wrong to value yourself, and women in general, based on their bodies rather then based on our other characteristics and traits. True beauty has little to do with one's physical appearance. Rather, beauty radiates from those who are self-accepting, confident about their special qualities and gifts, and open and compassionate toward others. All of us can become more beautiful by working hard to incorporate these positive elements into our lives.

> **Beauty is how you feel inside, and it reflects in your eyes. It is not something physical.**
>
> —Sophia Loren

What Makes Us Great

Many special qualities about women go far beyond our physical attributes. Unfortunately, not all of us are encouraged by our larger social environment to pursue and develop those qualities.

Males, in contrast, are often valued based on many attributes other than their appearance. We look to a man's intelligence, achievements, independence, athletic ability, and prestige in order to assess his worth. When people *do* focus on men's appearance, they are much less critical. When older men begin to get gray hair or develop wrinkles, they are sometimes called "distinguished." On the other hand, when older women develop the same signs of aging, they are expected to frantically begin trying anti-wrinkle creams, coloring their hair, and doing anything they can to look younger again. Because our culture does not value men and women based on similar standards and attributes, it is *our* responsibility to decide what makes us valuable.

> Self-empowerment —that's learning to respect other people's music, but dance to your own tune as you master harmony within yourself.
>
> —Doc Childre

Use this page to list what *you* think are some of the most important things about being a woman. If you like, under each word or phrase you list, draw a picture illustrating its meaning:

Many wonderful characteristics can be used to describe women. Women are often known for their intuition and insight and for their compassion toward others. Many women are described by their friends as good listeners and emotional support providers. Women who are moms often display great strength in their ability to withstand the challenges of childbirth, childrearing, and balancing complex lives filled with responsibilities and demands. Throughout time, many women have been brilliant scientists, dedicated leaders, and fierce activists.

List the names of three famous women who have made special accomplishments and describe what they are known for.

1.

2.

3.

In addition to all the characteristics described previously, women also have a lot of strength that is biologically based. On average, women are believed to have better physical endurance than men, and in general, women live longer than men. If we really want to focus on the strengths of women, we can go back even further than infancy: Sperm carrying female chromosomes out-swim male sperm. They live longer under unpleasant conditions in the womb and more frequently inseminate an egg to form a new fetus (which is why there is a larger population of women in the world). You probably have never thought about a woman's strength in those terms, right? And that's not all: in their development, girls take the lead by reading, talking, and counting earlier than boys, on average. They even tend to receive higher grades in elementary school than their male counterparts.

As we can see, there are many more important characteristics on which we can focus, rather than always preoccupying ourselves with how pretty we are or what our bodies look like! Women deserve a lot more credit, don't you think?

Let's learn some more about some of the most remarkable accomplishments achieved by women.

- **Jane Addams** (1860–1935) was a peace activist who worked throughout her life to provide help to the poor. She was the creator of Hull House in Chicago and founded the Women's International League for Peace and Freedom. Ms. Addams won the Nobel Peace Prize in 1931.

- **Tori Allen** (1988–) has been a world-renowned rock climber from the time she was a child. She spent her earlier years in a West African village, where she learned how to climb from her pet monkey, Georgia. By age 15 she had won several national and international junior championships, authored her first book, set a world climbing record in Yosemite, California, and was speaking to groups of youth about achieving excellence.

- **Linda G. Alvarado** (1952–) is a Latina businesswoman who started her own construction firm in 1976. She is the first Latina to own a major league baseball team: The Colorado Rockies Baseball Club.

- **Susan B. Anthony** (1820–1906) was a women's rights activist who, upon discovering that males were paid much more then females while working in the same jobs, helped build the women's rights movement. She was a pioneer in the struggle to earn women the right to vote.

- **Clara Barton** (1821–1912) founded the American Red Cross and became known as the "Angel of the Battlefield" because of her efforts to help injured soldiers during the Civil War.

- **Mary McLeod Bethune** (1875–1955) began a school to help educate African American women with only $1.50! Through her years of leadership, she worked to increase opportunities for African Americans and led the National Council of Negro Women.

- **Mary Steichen Calderone, MD** (1904–1998), developed sex education programming and was called the "mother of sex education." She started the Sexuality Information and Education Council of the United States.

- **Annie Jump Cannon** (1863–1941) was an astronomer who perfected the system that classifies stars. During her work at Harvard Observatory, she put together a larger amount of astronomical information than had ever been complied by another person!

- **Rachel Carson** (1907–1964), a zoologist, wrote a book called *Silent Spring* about pesticides and other poisons in our environment, that helped begin the environmental movement in the United States.

- **Donna De Varona** (1947–) became the youngest member of a U.S. Olympic swim team at 13 years old. Just four years later, she won two gold medals at the Tokyo Olympics. During her swimming career, she set 18 world records and became the first President of the Women's Sports Foundation in 1974. De Varona was the first full-time female sports broadcaster (for ABC).

- **Sylvia Earle** (1935–), an oceanographer, is internationally recognized as a leading marine biologist. She is the world's leading advocate to keep our seas safe, as they are the biggest and most important natural resource on the planet!

- **Shannon W. Lucid** (1943–), an astronaut, holds the international record for the most hours in space of any woman in the world. She has performed critical science experiments during her space voyages. Ms. Lucid was the first woman to receive the Congressional Space Medal of Honor.

- **Antonia Novello** (1944–) was the first woman and the first Latino to become the Surgeon General of the United States. She was one of the first authorities to focus on women and children with AIDS. As surgeon general, she also worked hard to fight against domestic violence and underage alcohol abuse.

- **Annie Oakley** (1860–1926) was an amazingly skilled target shooter and was likely the best in the nation. She gave much of her time and energy to helping other women by fighting for women's rights and was known across England and Europe for her incredible skills.

- **Sarah Winnemucca** (1842–1891) was the daughter of Chief Winnemucca of the Paiuts tribe in Nevada and California. She acted as a peacekeeper and bravely freed her father and other tribe members when they were held captive during the Bannock War in 1878. In advocating for the plight of her people, she gained the attention of President Hayes who promised to return her tribe to their land, the Malheur Reservation. The promise was never honored.

- **Chien-Shiung Wu** (1912–1997), a prominent physicist, made huge contributions to the study of atoms. She won many awards, including the Comstock Prize, which is given only once every five years. She was the first living scientist to have an asteroid named after her! (www.greatwomen.org).

It is normal to spend some of your time and energy focusing on the more day-to-day matters in life. Even women who have accomplished amazing things in their lives spend time pondering their physical appearance. But you can almost bet that the women we have just learned about spent much more time focused on what was truly most important about them, including their gifts, talents, and life purpose! It's amazing what we can accomplish when we really tune in to what is most special and important about us.

> I myself have never been able to find out precisely what feminism is; I only know that people call me a feminist whenever I express sentiments that differentiate me from a doormat.
> —Rebecca West

Now, consider your uniqueness as an individual by spending some time thinking and writing about the following:

What are some things you are good at—what are some of your gifts and talents?

What would some of the closest people in your life say are your best qualities?

Tell about an accomplishment or situation in which you felt proud of yourself:

Discuss a time in which you helped someone else and how you helped them:

What are the three things about yourself—not having to do with the way you look—that you would most like to work on or improve?

1.

2.

3.

How might you go about trying to improve or work on the things you listed?

Now consider the women who are most important in your life. Select one of them for a brief interview. Ask her if she could set aside some time so that you may ask her some questions about her experience of being a woman. If she agrees to be interviewed, ask her when would be a convenient time for the two of you to have some quiet privacy together. Pick a cozy spot and consider preparing a refreshing drink for you and your interviewee before you begin. When you are ready for your interview, ask the following questions:

What are some of the most significant ways—that are not physical—that you changed as you grew from a young girl into a woman?

What do you think are some of the most difficult things about being a woman?

What do you think are some of the most wonderful things about being a woman?

What has been your greatest life accomplishment?

Tell me a bit about a woman who has been influential in *your* life and how:

What is something you would like to learn to do?

Describe the three characteristics you possess that you are most proud of:

1.

2.

3.

Describe the three characteristics you possess that you would most like to change:

1.

2.

3.

What are some life lessons about being a woman that you want me to know?

chapter 16

Getting Over It!

Loving your body can be a very difficult task. It takes time to unlearn all the messages you have absorbed throughout your life about how women's bodies "should" look. Certainly, our culture does not always help women to feel proud of our bodies, no matter their size. Therefore, learning to feel good about your physical self is an exciting, even revolutionary act. Being able to move beyond obsessions with food and weight is a tremendous and important accomplishment.

Now let's look at ways that you can help yourself move into this new way of thinking on a daily basis, positively influencing your own body image and even becoming a role model for others.

- Educate yourself further about issues that affect women. The last section of this workbook is a list of suggested resource materials. Consider consulting your parent(s), caregiver, teacher, or another adult you trust to help you decide on materials that would be most appropriate for you.

> **Our ultimate freedom is the right and power to decide how anybody or anything outside ourselves will affect us.**
>
> —Steven Covey

125

- Compliment other young women on things other than their appearance. If you do this in front of boys or men, you will be modeling for the importance of recognizing qualities in girls and women other than the way they look.

- When you see ads that you think are negative, conscientiously choose to reject the messages they present and point out to your friends why you think the ad is harmful.

- Write letters to companies that feature negative ads and tell them you are not going to purchase whatever they are selling and why. Invite some girl-friends over and have your own "letter writing party," complete with a stack of magazines to look through, stationery, and stamps.

- Challenge yourself to participate in an activity that is usually reserved for boys. Ask a friend to join you. You may find a new favorite hobby!

- Limit the time you spend reading fashion magazines. If you'd like to read a teen magazine that does not have harmful ads, try *New Moon* magazine (contact information listed in reference section).

- Do nice things for your body, such as eating healthy foods, enjoying a bubble bath, giving yourself a foot massage, exercising, wearing comfortable clothes, and looking in the mirror to identify positive body traits.

- If you are harassed or treated disrespectfully or are made to feel uncom-fortable by someone, speak out immediately to an adult you trust. Keep talking until someone listens to you and offers their assistance.

> **Never doubt that a small group of thoughtful committed citizens can change the world. Indeed, it is the only thing that ever has.**
>
> **—Margaret Mead**

List some other ideas you can think of that may help you focus on achieving a healthier body image:

Remember, no one can make you feel inferior without your consent.

—Eleanor Roosevelt

Reflections of Your True Self

We receive lots of messages each day telling us what is expected of us as women. Over time, these messages can become so ingrained in our minds that we begin to believe that they are all true. When we allow ourselves to be taught only one perspective about who we should or should not be, we stop asking ourselves what we want. So here's a chance to think about what's important to you.

What traits are important for you to have to be happy, healthy, and successful?

A Look in the Mirror

What are some things you would like to do differently in your life to help you grow into an even stronger, healthier, and happier you?

What are some things you would like to keep doing the same?

What are three things explored in this workbook that you already knew about before you began?

1.

2.

3.

What are three things explored in this workbook that are new to you?

1.

2.

3.

Congratulations on all the hard work you have put into your workbook! By now, you have discovered that, like all people, you are constantly learning from the powerful messages present in your social environment. You have uncovered what some of these messages are and how they may impact you. Sometimes it will be difficult to decide whether certain messages may affect you positively or negatively. The most important thing, however, is that through this workbook, you have taken a critical first step in learning how to make conscious choices about which messages to accept into your life and which messages to reject. With this developing ability to shape your own learning, *you* will be in charge of your development, rather then allowing outside forces to tell you who to become.

As you become better able to shed negative messages and their harmful distractions of unrealistic beauty and thinness, you'll discover a whole world of interests that you may have been too preoccupied to enjoy before. This newfound freedom will help you pursue all that you love about life and living, leaving you better able to uncover your most valuable qualities and truest gifts.

In exploring who you are and who you wish to become, let your accomplishments here be reminder of your determination to be the best you possible. Use this experience to recall your own foundation of inner beauty, the qualities and interests you cherish most. And above all, may you always know the true worth of the woman reflecting back when you take *a look in the mirror.*

> We ask justice, we ask equality, we ask that all civil and political rights that belong to the citizens of the United States be guaranteed to us and our daughters forever.
>
> —Susan B. Anthony

For More Information

Below you will find resources: books, magazines, videos, and websites that can provide you with more information about the issues you explored in this workbook. Consider involving an adult you trust—a parent, caregiver, librarian, or teacher—in reviewing the list, helping you select the most appropriate materials for you, and helping you find more resources if you need them.

Books

Bolden, T. (1998). *33 things every girl should know.* New York: Crown.

Boston Women's Health Book Collective. (1998). *Our bodies, ourselves: For the new century.* New York: Simon & Schuster, Inc.

Brumberg, J. J. (1997). *The body project: An intimate history of American girls.* New York: Vintage.

Carlip, H. (1996). *Girl power: Young women speak out.* New York: Warner Books, Inc.

Igus, T., with D. Patrick. (1992). *Great women in the struggle, Vol 2: An intro for young readers.* East Orange, NJ: Just Us Books.

Jackson, D., (1992). *How to make the world a better place for women in five minutes a day.* New York: Hyperion.

Maine, M. (1991). *Father hunger: Fathers, daughters, and food.* Carlsbad, CA: Gurze Books.

Miller, M. (1997). *An intricate weave: Women write about girls and girlhood.* Laguna Beach, CA: Iris Editions.

Odean, K. (1997). *Great books for girls: More than 600 books to inspire today's girls and tomorrow's women.* New York: Ballantine Books.

Pipher, M. (1995). *Reviving Ophelia: Saving the selves of adolescent girls.* New York: Ballantine Books.

Pipher, M. (1997). *Hunger pains: The modern woman's tragic quest for thinness.* New York: Ballantine Books.

Pohlman, S., Boyles, D., & Turner, P. (1997). *A girl's guide to life: The complete instructions, written by kids for kids.* New York: Penguin.

Rimm, S. (1999). *See jane win.* New York: Crown.

Seid, R. P. (1989). *Never too thin: Why women are at war with their bodies.* New York: Prentice Hall Press.

Wolf, N. (1991). *The beauty myth: How images of beauty are used against women.* New York: William Morrow & Company.

Magazines

Dream/Girl Magazine
P.O. Box 97365
Raleigh, NC 27624
www.dgArts.com

New Moon Magazine
New Moon Publishing
800/381-4743
www.newmoon.org

Radiance; The Magazine for Large Women
510/885-1505
www.radiancemagazine.com

Teen Voices Magazine
Women Express, Inc.
888/882-TEEN
www.teenvoices.com

Videos

BodyTalk 1
BodyTalk 2
The Body Positive
2550 Ninth St, Suite 204B
Berkeley, CA 94710
510-548-0101
www.thebodypositive.org

A Hero for Daisy
A Hero for Daisy, Inc.
P.O. Box 81005
Wellesley Hills, MA 02481
877/98-DAISY
www.aherofordaisy.com

Still Killing Us Softly
(Dr. Jean Kilbourne, 1979)
Cambridge Documentary Films, Inc.
617/484-3996

Websites

www.adiosbarbie.com
www.agirlsworld.com
www.aliveness.net
www.anincomeofherown.com
www.chabotspace.org/visit/programs/techbridge.asp
www.cybergrrl.com
www.dadsanddaughters.org
www.dgarts.com
www.genderequity.org
www.genderwatchers.org
www.girlpower.gov/girlarea/index.htm
www.girlpower.com
www.girlstart.com
www.girlzone.com

www.gurl.com
www.i-glow.com
www.indiegurl.com
www.motm.org
www.smartgirl.com
www.teenconnection.org
www.thebodypositive.org
www.turnbeautyinsideout.org
www.vtc.vsc.edu
www.yourexpedition.com
www.youthexpressions.org

Author's References

Apostolides, M. (1998). *Inner hunger.* New York: W.W. Norton & Company, Inc.

Beaumont, A. (2000-2001). *Corseting the human body.* Retrieved February 2004 from www.staylace.com/medicaladvice/med4cthb.htm.

Boston Women's Health Book Collective. (1998). *Our bodies, ourselves: For the new century.* New York: Simon & Schuster, Inc.

Brumberg, J. J. (1988). *Fasting girls: The emergence of anorexia nervosa as a modern disease.* Cambridge, MA: Harvard University Press.

Brumberg, J. J. (1997). *The body project: An intimate history of American girls.* New York: Vintage.

Bureau For At-Risk Youth. (1995). *Last pick...Self esteem and body image* (From the Working it out at Madison High video series). Plainview, NY: At-Risk Resources. Item # VD 381 C2 30162; available from 800/99-YOUTH.

Bureau For At-Risk Youth. (n. d.). *Self-image: The fantasy, the reality* (The Mix for Teens by Teens video series). Plainview, NY: At-Risk Resources. Item #VD 405 S7 31494; available from 800/99-YOUTH.

Bureau For At-Risk Youth. (n. d.). *Thea's mirror: A parent's guide to helping teens with eating disorders.* (From the Parenting Difficult Adolescents video series.) Plainview, NY: At-Risk Resources. Item # VD 362 E2 30137; available from 800/99-YOUTH.

Claude-Pierre, P. (1997). *The secret language of eating disorders.* New York: Random House.

French, M. (1992). *The war against women.* New York: Summit Books.

Friday, N. (1993). *The power of beauty.* New York: HarperCollins.

Gruver, Nancy (2004). *How to say It to girls: Communicating with your growing daughter.* New York: Prentice Hall.

Hoffman, E. (1993). *Our health, our lives: A revolutionary approach to total health care for women.* New York: Simon & Schuster, Inc.

Jackson, D. (1992). *How to make the world a better place for women in five minutes a day.* New York: Hyperion.

Kelly, J. (2002). *Dads and daughters: How to inspire, understand, and support your daughter when she's growing up so fast.* New York: Broadway.

Kilbourne, J. (1979). *Still Killing Us Softly.* Cambridge, MA: Cambridge Documentary Films, Inc. (617/484-3996).

Marone, N. (1998). *How to mother a successful daughter: A practical guide to empowering girls from birth to eighteen.* New York: Random House.
(Ms. Marone is also the author of *How to father a successful daughter.*)

Pipher, M. (1995). *Reviving Ophelia: Saving the selves of adolescent girls.* New York: Ballantine Books.

Pipher, M. (1997). *Hunger pains: The modern woman's tragic quest for thinness.* New York: Ballantine Books.

Pipher, M. (1997). *The shelter of each other: Rebuilding our families.* New York: Ballantine Books.

Rimm, S. (1999). *See Jane win.* New York: Crown.

Seid, R. P. (1989). *Never too thin: Why women are at war with their bodies.* New York: Prentice Hall Press.

Thomas, L. (1997). *10 essential foods: A sensible, good-humored approach to vitality, health and well-being.* Prescott, AZ: Hohm Press.

Weil, A. (2000). *Eating well for optimum health: The essential guide to food, diet and nutrition.* New York: Alfred A. Knopf.

Wells, D. (1994). *Getting there: The movement toward gender equality.* New York: Carroll & Graf.

Wolf, N. (1991). *The beauty myth: How images of beauty are used against women.* New York: William Morrow & Co.

National Organizations and Websites

Women's College Coalition
125 Michigan Avenue, NE
Washington, DC 20017
202/234-0443
www.academic.org

The Aliveness Experience
Box 1591
Lake Grove, OR 97035
503/293-8906
www.aliveness.net

The Body Positive
2550 Ninth St, Suite 204B
Berkeley, CA 94710
510-548-0101
www.thebodypositive.org

Mind on the Media
710 St. Olaf Ave. Suite 200
Northfield, MN 55057
952/210-1625
www.motm.org

The National Women's Hall of Fame
76 Fall Street, P.O. Box 335
Seneca Falls, NY 13148
315/568-8060
www.greatwomen.org

National Eating Disorders Association
603 Stewart St., Suite 803
Seattle, WA 98101
206/382-3587
www.nationaleatingdisorders.org

TV-Turnoff Network
1200 29th Street NW, Lower Level #1
Washington, DC 20007
202/333-9220
www.tv-turnoff.org

www.kidshealth.org

www.mysistahs.org

www.teenpuberty.com

About the Author

Valerie R. McManus (formerly Valerie Lasoff), LCSW-C, is a licensed clinical social worker practicing in Maryland. Ms. McManus obtained her Masters in Social Work at the University of Maryland at Baltimore, where she worked with the Legal Aid Bureau's Nursing Home Program and as an intern therapist at the St. Vincent's Group Home for Children. Since obtaining her MSW, she has worked as a treatment foster care worker, providing clinical assistance to families and children with special needs. She continues her work in child welfare as a part-time case supervisor for Anne Arundel County's Court-Appointed Special Advocates program (CASA, Inc.) in Annapolis, Maryland, and she has a women-focused private therapy practice in Odenton, Maryland. Ms. McManus resides in Odenton, Maryland, with her husband Craig and their yellow Labrador, Willow.